Introduction

I'll open with an admission: I am not a fan of motivational writing or motivational videos or any of those damned cliched motivational quotations.

Have you ever been really hungry for food and drank a glass of water? I have. Water is good for me, but it kind of makes me mad at that moment because it's the last thing I want when I'm hungry for food. That's how I feel when reading or listening to the tried-and-true motivational sayings that we all know.

So the first thought I had when creating The Mirror of Motivation was to make sure that this book was devoid of all of that cookie-cutter rah-rah shit.

What is universal for any form of motivational writing are the principles -- we all want to feel good. We all want to be happy and content with what we have produced in our lives. Most of us, I think, would love to do even better -- however you define *better* -- than we do now. This book will put you in position to *put you in position*, mentally, to go out and do just that.

All of us have to come up with ways to motivate ourselves. It's the Law of Inertia -- some stimulus must act as the catalyst between us sitting on our asses and taking the initiative to actual do something, anything, to get what or to where we want.

We are all wired differently, though. The thoughts or words or songs that get me going are not the same things, necessarily, that will work for you. Which is why this book is the Mirror -- The Mirror of Motivation is about the motivational tools within and around *you*, and exactly how to tap into and exploit them. Because you can't depend on a book to fuel you forever, let this book train you to do it for yourself.

This book is a collection of principles I've come to learn in my life. Some are thoughts I came up with through simply tossing them around in my mind over and over. Some may have been sparked by something someone else -- whom I may or may not know -- said or did. My goal with this book is to build on the aforementioned principles and picked-up thoughts and efforts, and leave the world in better shape for me having been here.

This is not a how-to book. I have never believed that getting people to change their behaviors permanently can come from telling someone to "Do this, that, and this." Permanent change takes place when a person has their beliefs changed through their own thinking and experience. Telling someone to change how they think, is ineffective in the long run -- they may agree for the moment and even understand on the surface, but people will only change their beliefs and actions when they tell themselves to, not when they are told to. This book is not a tell-me-what-to-do book. This book will place you, mentally, in a space where you will look at yourself, your thoughts and actions and decide what the difference is between where/who/what you are and where/who/what you want to be.

Then you will stop reading, thinking and talking, and go *fucking do it*.

So this book will ask you many questions. Questions that I am not asking you for answers to -- the answers are for you to tell yourself, and no one else. The answers to the questions asked of you in this book are designed to make you think about what you do and why you do it, what you think, why you think it and how those thoughts drive your (in)actions. Be honest with yourself -- this is a **Mirror**, after all. Mirrors never lie. If you don't like what you see in a mirror, there is no one to blame and no rationalizing. If you don't like your answers, start by changing your thoughts. This will lead to a change in actions and overall qualitative change in your life. What that change will be, is your choice. That's all there is to it.

Here goes.

Looking For Tips?   8
Stick With It.   9
What You're Up Against.   10
Know Your Goals.   11
How Much Time Should I Put In Daily?   13
Talent Vs. Skills. 14
If You Reached Your Highest Goal Tomorrow, Would You Be Ready For It?   15
Self Discipline.   16
What Do You Need To Be Good At? 17
Make Your Own Decisions.   18
Think Like The Best, Be The Best. 19
Are You Being Realistic?   20
Work On Your Game. 21
Finishing Strong. 22
What If You Got A Second Chance? 23
Go Out And Live.   24
Wei Wu Wei (Do Without Doing): Stop Thinking And Just Do It.   25
Want More Luck? Show Up More.   26
Ready To Face The Best? 27
Use Your Pain As Motivation.   28
Make Plans Bigger Than Yourself.   29
Haters & Naysayers. 30
Are You Ready For Your Future Competition?   31
Consistency Of Effort.   32
Think Of What You Have -- Not What You Don't Have.   33
Do You Believe You? 34
Bring A Competitive Mentality. You'll Need It.   35
Everything You Want, Wants You.   36
Picking Yourself Up Mentally.   37
Confidence Is Everything. 38
Be Who You Are. 39
Practice Your Belief. 40
Don't Seek Approval. 41
As Long As Your Mind Still Sees It, It's Possible.   42
Crush Your Opposition.   43
Don't Worry About What Anyone Else Is Doing.   44
Find Inspiring Influences. 45
Value Your Time. 46
Appreciate Yourself. 47
Focus on What You Can Control.   48
Fundamentals First.   49
Bad Or Good: Whatever You Make It.   50

Get Advice Only From Those Who Have Done It. 51
You Are Either Building or Destroying.   52
If You're Really Working It Will Show.   53
Recognize Your Calling.   54
5 Keys: Work. Focus. Study. Stick To It. Believe.   55
Be Willing To Stand Alone.   56
Have A Bad Memory. 57
Outside Motivation Only Goes So Far. Is It In You?   58
Check Yourself.   59
Use What You've Got. 60
Take Care of Business.   61
Be An Opportunist: Embrace and Make the Most of Your Situation. 62
Be Your Own #1 Fan. 63
Relax Your Mind. (Meditation) 64
Life is Short. Do It Now.   65
Better to Do It Than Not Do It.   66
Keep Positive Reminders Around You.   67
Where's Your Energy Going?   68
You Only Need To Be Right Once.   69
Be The Boss of Your Organization. 70
Greatness Makes No Excuses. 71
Give Yourself Permission To Fail.   72
Easy Success Tip: Show Up.   73
Defeat The Negativity.   74
Who's Around You, Who Wants You Around? 75
Walk Away in Strength, Not Weakness. 76
What You Think, Attracts More of It.   77
Be Real With Yourself.   78
Someone Above You Is Doing Something You're Not Doing.   79
No One Can "Make You Feel" Anything. 80
The "Super You." 81
Visualize Your Future.   82
People Will Always Criticize.   83
Persistence: Boring But Necessary. 84
Be, Do, Have.   85
Being Self-Generated.   86
Erase The Bad Movies.   87
Surround Yourself With People Who Can Help You.   88
You Learn by Doing, Over and Over.   89
You "Need Help"? 90
You Already Have All You Need.   91
You Don't Need More "How-To."   92
Make The Difficult Easy, and The Easy Difficult. 93

Know Everything About Your Work. 94
Help Others, It Will Come Back To You. 95

Looking For Tips?

When I first started putting basketball training videos on YouTube with some level of consistency, I was bombarded with requests from players who wanted some insight into improving their performance. Funny thing was, no one was asking anything specific -- just, "Tips on getting better." I was sick of the word "tips" in 2008. So after one after-hours workout I put my feelings on camera and *"Work On Your (Fuckin') Game"* was born.

The best tip you can get when it pertains to your work is just what I said: Work On Your Game. Some people are waiting in vain for that one magic tip that will take them over the top or make them rich or miraculously have them performing at the level they say they so badly want to be at. Some people think there is some secret, hidden information out there that they just don't have access to.

And they're right. I'll share that secret information with you right now:

When you put your head down and focus on the process of doing the work instead of looking for four-leaf clovers, results will come. If someone is doing better than you, and they are in the same arena you are in, that person is doing something that you're not doing (more on this later). There are some exceptions, but it's likely that that something is, they are working more and harder than you are. When you're resting, taking days off, watching reality shows, reading gossip blogs, they are putting in the work. When you're taking it easy at work they are pushing themselves past comfort.

No YouTube videos or motivational books or music or famous people on TV can help you get better. **You must help yourself**. How do you think those people in the videos, writing the books, smiling on the television screen, got there?

Ask anyone who is very good or great at something about how they got to their   current level. Some answers will be long, some short. One universal attribute of each of those people's success, though, will be: "I put in the work. Even now, I still put in the work."

If you do not read another page of this book, you have all the information you need.

Stick With It.

It takes time -- a lot of time -- to become a master at any craft (this sentence alone will scare off half of your competition, if it doesn't scare *you* off). A long period of focused, on-purpose work. Few people reach the master level at anything in life because they move on to the next fresh, exciting thing as soon as their original choice gets too hard or too boring or they get discouraged from looking at others who are better than they are at that point.

News Flash: On your journey to mastery there will be boring days (many of them). You will have days when you'd rather go back to sleep (most people *will* go back to sleep). You will see people accomplishing more than you with seemingly less effort, leading to the poor-me mindset, or thoughts of outright quitting. You'll think you are doing something wrong.

Other activities will flirt with your focus and attention. Think of all these stimuli as a sort of filter that everyone on your same path must go through. The Filter is slick and resourceful. It can change form from thoughts that weaken your resolve to juicy distractions that break your focus. The Filter always shows up when you are at your weakest point, and it always comes bearing gifts as whatever might pull you away from your long-term goal. Which filter will weed **you** out of the race?

It's been said that any human being can have anything he wants as long as he is willing to ask 1,000 people for it, man of whom will say no. How many "No" answers can you tolerate before you quit? Many only last through two or three "No's" and its over.

Read the backstory of any successful person in any area of life, and they all will have a point in their story at which they could (and, most would have told them at that point, *should*) have quit. Odds were against them and a myriad of challenges piled up at once. They felt weak and alone, and the simple resolution would be to pack it up, lower their ambitions and go to where it was safe. But that story wouldn't be a story if they had walked away at that point. That is the difference between a success story, and the story of a person who was momentarily good but faded away, leaving us asking, "Whatever happened to _____?" You can fill in the blank, I'm sure, with plenty of names from a bunch of different areas of life.

The real question is, what are you willing to do to make sure you are not the name in that blank for someone down the road?

What You're Up Against.

The world of human beings as we know it is much bigger than you think. In the time it takes you to read this sentence, there are more people in existence than there were before you started the sentence. Humans aren't dying as fast as new humans are being born. This means that every day, someone new is entering the same lane you're in, and they want your spot, even if they don't know it -- **you** know it now.

Your luck can change fast in this world -- one instance of unpreparedness could be your golden opportunity blowing away in the wind. And one day of being ready -- not because you knew opportunity was coming, but just because you chose to be ready -- might be your big day. You don't know when or even if that day is coming. So, decide if its worth it to always be ready or not. If not, somebody out there will gladly do what you won't.

The world is a very big place. Think about how many people in the world are aiming to do the same thing you're aiming to do; there are likely more of them than you estimate. Getting into a certain university. Starting a business. Making a sports team or league.

This information is not intended to discourage you or have you reconsider your goals. What you need to do, however, is reconsider how committed you are to making it happen and reassess what it will take for you to rise above the rest. Because "the rest" is a lot of people.

Know Your Goals.

At around age seventeen I decided I wanted to be a great basketball player. My less-than-modest basketball success to that date encouraged me, because I had began in basketball not even able to perform the basic functions of the game. I knew I could do it, though, because even then, I had a clear vision of what I was to become. I could see it and I could feel it. I knew the world was a lot bigger than my Mt. Airy neighborhood in Philly. So it wasn't about beating this guy or that guy in one-on-one or scoring some number of points in a pickup game. I wanted to, one day, look at all the players around me from back then and know I had taken my basketball life further than any of them. So at every level that I approached, I envisioned what I was going to do before I began.

My visions: I would make the varsity team at my high school to shut up all the people at my neighborhood park who said I'd never make it. I would to go to college and make the team at college, which alone would put my career accomplishments above many of the streetball players I grew up playing against. At college, I saw myself impressing everyone from the beginning of the first semester -- the preseason pickup games -- and validating my skills since my high school playing resume wasn't impressive. As a college player, I knew that making the pros after college would elevate me above all the college teammates who would never play in a single professional game.

I envisioned all of those things before they happened and those visions drove me to where I eventually went.

Say you want to lose weight. You need a vision for your weight loss that is more specific than simple "lose weight". Such as, How much weight? What do you want to look like? What will it feel like? When you run into a person you haven't seen in five years, how will they react to your transformation?

Say you want to score more points in basketball. How many more? How will you score those points? What impact will your performance have on your team and opponents?

You want more female attention. Which females? What will you do when that pretty girl who used to ignore you is now staring your way? How will you approach her? *Will* you approach her?

You want to make more money. How much more exactly? What will you do with it, where will you go? How will your lifestyle change?

It's good and necessary to work, but without a goal or vision, how will you know when your work is done? How will you know if your work was/is sufficient? You need a target to aim at. When your targets are clear in front of you, you can see what's working and what's not, and you can change your goals or your plans if necessary. Decide what you want to do, then decide in detail. Some people prescribe coming up with specific and measurable ways to know you've reached your goals, which works. You can also use the technique I used in my teen years: There were no numbers or charts, but there was a very a clear vision of how things would be, how I'd feel.

Think about the big picture and long term of your life and where you want to be in ten years. A hunter with no deer to shoot is just a wild man with a gun.

How Much Time Should I Put In Daily?

If you're ever asking this question, it's time to step back and reassess what you're doing and why you're doing it.

First off, if you're doing something that you chose to be doing, you need not be told how much time to put into it -- you decided to do it, why does it matter how much time you're spending on it? If you believe in something, you eat, drink and sleep it; there's no clocking out. And the time you spend on it is all in the name of the result that you're after, not in patting yourself on the back because you worked for three hours yesterday.

Second, your work -- work that you have chosen -- is not measured in time. We all have 24 hours per day, no matter how old or young, new or experienced. The work you do and the results you produce -- not the clock -- are the measuring sticks of your efforts.

The only place you should be watching the clock is at the 9-5 job you don't really like. Outside of this, if you are watching the clock while working on something you chose to work on, as if a certain amount of time spent makes you successful or will gain you acceptance, you need to find something else to do. If you have a certain time window before other commitments require your presence, determine what you need to get done within the allotted time each day or session. Untie yourself from the "time = work" myth.

Production and results are your boss, not the clock. It's not the time you spend working that counts, it's what you get out of that time that counts.   If you need to measure, set an output/results goal, not a time goal.

Talent Vs. Skills.

By definition, talent is "natural ability that exists without effort or practice."

Skill is "practiced ability that we consciously acquire."

We all have talents; some have more than others. All talents, however, have a finite supply and talent cannot be bought.

Reality of Life: Some people will have more talent than you have in certain areas. Skills are for sale, though, paid for through effort. Put in enough focused effort for enough time and your skills will increase. No amount of efforts can add to your talent -- you have what you have and that's it. Skill, however, is for sale daily on the open market at a fixed price. And the price never changes.

What we see and identify as talent is usually a habit of consistent effort that led to a high level of skill. Refined, polished skills, in the eyes of someone who did not see the work done to acquire such skills, looks like what we know as talent. Labeling what we see as "talent" makes us feel better about ourselves: they were just born with that ability, we tell ourselves. If we saw if for what it really is -- skills -- then there is no excuse for us to make when we look in the mirror. That internal conversation leads to tough questions we'd have to ask ourselves that we really don't wish to address. Thus, that skill we see in others gets labeled as "talent."

There will always be people who will avoid that conversation and label the skill they see as talent. Knowing this, there is nothing stopping you from becoming the person being talked about in the above scenario, as opposed to being the one explaining the proficiency of the observed.

Your skill level doesn't have a ceiling -- more practice and work equals more skills. You can go and get it as long as you are willing to pay the price.

If You Reached Your Highest Goal Tomorrow, Would You Be Ready For It?

Whatever your highest goal is right now, imagine you reached it tomorrow.

Have you been taking the proper actions to even make this a possibility?

Are you prepared for this position?

Could you maintain it (your current habits would determine this)?

Would you feel you belonged there, if you woke up there tomorrow (are you mentally prepared)?

Are there any differences between the person you are right now, and the person you'd need to be at the pinnacle of your goals (what are you not doing)?

What do you need to do to close that gap?

What are you going to do today to make progress on closing that gap?

Usually the difference between where you are and where you want to be is not what you do, the difference is who you are. Become that goal.

Self Discipline.

The true test of your commitment comes when there is no one watching over you, no one to answer to, no one forcing you to work. What will you do with that freedom?

A person I worked for in college once told me that his employees never did what he expected of them. But, his employees *always* did what he *inspected*. Because, those employees knew, the inspected work was going to be checked over and the employee would be held directly accountable.

Would you work the same, under nothing more than your own expectations, as you would if there was a boss inspecting your output?

If you do a half-assed job, do you call yourself out on it and make sure to get it done properly, or let it pass because no one is watching?

Do you show up at the same time every day and get to work like you would expect of your favorite coffee or doughnut shop (this is also know as being a professional)?

If you weren't you and you watched yourself -- your actions, your habits, your disciplines -- for a week, what kind of business would you see Yourself, Inc. as?

You can't expect your life to be dictated and watched over by another person forever if you plan to have any power in this world. You have to discipline yourself to do things correctly, how and when they need to be done.

What Do You Need To Be Good At?

Whatever your line of work, there are certain skills that you need to be able to perform at a high level. It is just as important to know how to do them as it is to know what they are.

For your situation, do you know what you need to be very good at? If you're just starting out and you don't know, this is okay -- we call this "not knowing what you don't know." Now it's time to find out.

If you've been in your line of work for some time now and you don't know what you must be good at in that line of work, it's time to wake up. If you don't know, new or old to the job, there are resources -- books, the Internet, people. Ask around and talk to others who do the same thing you do. Watch and observe people in action. Read -- there is a book or blog out there, somewhere, with the exact information that you want, waiting to be consumed.

The fundamentals of your field is the base you build on. Without it, your building crumbles.

Make Your Own Decisions.

There are many tough choices ahead of you. Questions of who, what, when, where, and how that will have to be answered. Who will you become? How will you handle and present yourself in new places and to new people? Which direction should you take your life when you reach the many inevitable crossroads in life? Which pair of shoes to wear tomorrow?

The tendency of some people is to seek advice. Advice is what we ask for when we already know the answer and just want to hear someone else validate it. Another option is to have someone else tell you what you should do or what the best move is. The issue with that way of thinking is, no one else is you. No one else has ever had a situation exactly the same as yours. Another person can tell you what to do and what your best options would be, but that person is speaking from their own perspective. When you ask another person what is best for you, that person is speaking as they see things, not as you see them. There are intricacies and nuances in your life that even the closest friend or family member will never understand.

Understand that life is an accumulation of decisions. Look at your life right now: it is made completely of the decisions you've made up to this point. Your future will reflect the decisions you are making right now. Is there a person out there who you want deciding your future, or would you prefer to handle that yourself? You have only one life and only you have to live it, so take control and make the decisions that will shape it.

Think Like The Best, Be The Best.

One of my favorite authors, named Tucker Max, once told a story from his high school years. Tucker was on the basketball team, and his coach, weary from telling his players over and over what they were doing wrong, wanted to show them. So the coach created an assignment: For that day only, each player had to conduct himself in practice as if he were a different player on the team. This way, each player could see how he looked through his teammate's eyes. Tucker happened to get assigned to mimic the guy who was the best player on the basketball team.

According to Tucker, Tucker played basketball on that one day in practice, better than he had ever played before, or since.

Tucker's story shows what happens when a person "fools" their self into believing they are someone other than who they habitually are, or even a greater version of themselves. What's great for all of us is that this is not really a trick; when you can get yourself into a certain mindset and really believe it, and act on it, it is all very real.

The human brain is literal. Meaning, everything fed to it is taken at face value. The brain is not capable of differentiating between real life and fantasy and does not understand negation (telling yourself "don't trip up these stairs" is a message to your brain to focus on tripping on the stairs). What that means is, whatever information you feed to your brain, and really feel and believe in it, your brain believes it. If you tell your brain,

"I am the best player on this team," your brain agrees and you body will follow the brain's instructions.

For Tucker Max, when that day of practice was over and he told himself, "OK, show's over. Go back to being your normal self. I'm not the best player on the team anymore," he went back to being the mediocre player he had been before that day.

It was easy for Tucker to temporarily be the best player that day because someone told him to do it and it was fun to try for a day. The hard part for all of us is tricking ourselves in this manner when no one cares whether you do it or not, or for how long, which is, for most of us, 99% of our lives. Do it enough, and believe it enough, and it becomes your normal way of being. The people you look up to or see as stars are regular folk just like you and me; they simply mastered the habit of tapping into that belief to the point that they know no other way of being. This doesn't cost money and no one can do it for you. Once you tap into it, no one can stop you.

Are You Being Realistic?

"Being realistic" is a phrase I've never heard come out of the mouth of a five-year-old. "Realistic" is a term we adopt as we grow into adults, used to rationalize unmet desires and goals we have come to deem unreachable. The fact is, "Realistic" is a relative term; what is not possible in the mind of one person is perfectly reasonable, even expected, in the mind of another.

Usually, "Being realistic" is thrown around by people who are negating a possible thought or action. "Be realistic, you can't do that." "You're asking a lot. Be realistic."

I cannot recall hearing the "realistic" directive being used to lift someone's expectations or actions. "That's all you think you're capable of? Be realistic!" "Of course you can date her. C'mon, be realistic!"

"Realistic" has come to be used as a hammer to tramp down your lofty ideas.

Reject this.

You and only you can decide what is realistic for you. And you have the mental power to change that reality, right now.

Work On Your Game.

Whatever your craft, you have to put in the work to perfect your skills. Once you've reached that high level you have to work twice as hard not only to maintain it, but for the competitors gunning for you up on that pedestal. If you're going to be the best at something and remain in that position, know now that the work will not end unless you decide to fall or be knocked down from your perch. And that fall will be hard.

Great writers, award winning artists, and champion swimmers work on their craft a lot more than everyone else in their fields. They may make it seem easy and effortless. We humans, unable to shoulder the tiring mental task of looking beneath the exterior of everything presented to us, generally accept what we see -- deciding that it's just natural for them. Believing this fallacy gives us a pass to ignore the fact that we just haven't put the work in at something to reach that highest level. This protects our fragile human egos.

Perfect timing, or knowing the right person, or some other random happenstance could create an opportunity for you any day now. How would you feel to miss that opportunity because you were not prepared enough to take advantage of it? What feeling could be worse? I'd rather do all the work and be over-prepared for wherever I end up, than have the opportunity to get all I want in front of me and miss it because I wasn't ready.

Doing the work is all you can control; changing circumstances can effect the overall outcome of anything you do. The act of putting in the effort, truly and consistently, will transfer to the next thing you take on, and the next thing after that. Effort is a habit.

Some people think there is some secret to a high level of achievement that is somehow being kept secret from them. This belief gives us an excuse to not do what we all know we need to do if we are to reach those lofty goals: Work.

Finishing Strong.

The last act, the way things finish, is what people remember. You did all that hard work and you deserve the credit and goodwill that naturally accompany a job well done. The way things end lingers on in the mind of everyone involved. That ending sets the table, so to speak, for future encounters. What do your table settings of endings read like? Are there sour, bitter tastes (i.e., something or someone you probably can't go back to and/or call on again)? Incomplete table settings (awkward endings with no closure)? How many full settings did you leave in your past -- situations that can be reopened, people you can call on years later, memories that bring a smile to your face? The way things end determines the table setting.

Finish what you start. Do not make mistakes of carelessness in your haste to move on to the next thing, messing up all of your hard work to this point. A strong finish leaves everyone satisfied. As my trainer says when I'm doing sprints, don't run *to* the finish line, run *through* the finish line.

What If You Got A Second Chance?

Think of a situation in your life that didn't go quite right. Really take some time to recall details and how everything transpired. Feel the feelings you felt back then, then feel the thoughts of what you could have done differently if you knew then what you know now.

What if you went back and got a second chance at it? A chance to make that situation right? Are you, in your present state, prepared and capable of doing that? Are you in better shape now, mentally or physically or emotionally, than you were back then?

Put that situation on your mind today. Not for purposes of beating yourself up over a past regret or conjuring up negative feelings, because we can never go back, but as fuel to be ready and able when another opportunity presents itself today. You never know when one will be right in front of you. In this mind state you won't miss, or be unprepared for, anything again.

Go Out And Live.

Books are great (especially this one). So is the Internet. TV was a great invention. I don't play video games but I understand the enjoyment derived from them.

However, there is only so far you can go with these devices when it comes to making your life what you want it to be. Life is out there, waiting for people to come and live it. Many people live their best lives in their imaginations, burying their active thoughts in television, magazines, websites and fantasies about what and who they could be.

Life, however, is in the actions -- interaction, experiences. Thinking about, or watching something is not equal to doing it. You probably have seen that there are a lot more people talking about doing things that they have never experienced, than those who have really done them, talking about it. Why is this? Because those who have done it have moved on to doing the next thing -- life continues. We cannot live off our pasts.

Your greatest accomplishment is history, even if it happened five minutes ago. Every passing minute, that accomplishment gets older and more outdated. What are you going to do next? What are you doing now? How will you live moving forward?

If you want life you have to go where the living is: the present, the here and now.

Are you living?

Wei Wu Wei (Do Without Doing): Stop Thinking And Just Do It.

Have you ever been walking and turned your conscious thought to the act of walking? What happened? There's a good chance that you slowed down or misstepped, tripped or stumbled for no reason. What about tying your shoes or brushing your teeth? If you stop and actually think about these actions as you do them the chances of messing up or doing things backwards increases, because these muscle-memorized, hard-wired activities are done best when we put them on auto pilot.

Many of our physical activities are best done unconsciously; that is, without actively thinking about what we're doing as we do it. When we put too much conscious thought towards our autopilot activities, we mess them up.

Wei Wu Wei, "the action of non-action," is a Taoist principle of doing things without letting our oversize human brains get in the way. Thinking is a process that takes time and energy. Thinking is a good thing in many instances. In the heat of an action that we have practiced over and over, however, the time to think is over. After a routine or skill has been drilled into you, there is no need to think about it -- like tying your shoes. If you think about tying your shoes, you slow down because your complex mind, on every movement, will ask, "What are we doing? Why? How?"

In the time it takes the mind to formulate and deliver and answer, your unconscious mind, powered by muscle memory, would have finished already. In this way, thinking everything out is not always necessary nor the best option. Thinking requires hesitation. There are moments in life that call for swift, bold action, no stopping to hem and haw and consider.

You know what you have practiced and what actions you don't need to stop and tell yourself how to do because they are drilled into you. Let your mind go and just do them, without conscious thought. As jazz great Charlie Parker once said, "Master the instrument, master the music, then forget all that shit and play."

Want More Luck? Show Up More.

Luck is a combination of readiness meeting opportunity. What we call luck -- some random, good thing happening to us -- is not really random at all. Opportunity is everywhere, it's just that we find ourselves unprepared to take advantage. And even when we are prepared, those opportunities can't meet your readiness if you're not around. So you have to make a point of showing up more often, which alone increases the chances of something good happening to or for you.

A "professional" is not defined by money or status of the length of her contract. As trainer Cus D'Amato told Mike Tyson in Tyson's early boxing days, a professional is someone who goes out and performs, every time, no matter what he's feeling on the inside. Showing up every day is not an action you do, it's a lifestyle. It's who you are. And being who you are, whomever you choose to be, is not luck.

Ready To Face The Best?

Who's the best in your field, in your area, in your office, on your team? If you had to face them today, head to head, with your job or position on the line, would you be ready to compete? Can you win? Do you think you can win? Regardless of outcome, would you earn respect? Why or why not?

You can only be amongst the best by going up against the best. Even if the opportunity to face them is not available in your current circumstance, use this idea to keep yourself on-point mentally. Being on top is a way of being, a habit, a trait of a person's character. If you prepared as if you're playing for the championship belt tomorrow, what would you not be ready for?

Are you ready to measure your skills with or against those who are at the top of your field?

If yes, you better stay prepared, mentally and physically. If not, you need to get it together, and fast.

Use Your Pain As Motivation.

We all experience pain. Setbacks happen, bad days occur. You didn't do your best. Someone let you down. Some random circumstance interrupts your plans. It's happened to all of us and it will happen again.

You have a choice of how to deal with all of these things, and you have the choice of being active in this choosing. Pain can debilitate you and paralyze you into inaction: Why even put forth the effort if everything goes wrong? This is the mindset that crystallizes when you allow your pain to take control of your mind in a negative way.

Pain can also be transformed into fuel that gives you the energy to keep going. If the things you do all seem to come easy and you don't face walls in your path, you are likely living within your comfort zone and going nowhere. The pain you feel as setbacks and adversity is merely a challenge to see how much you really want to make something happen; how much effort you're really willing to put in. Every ounce of pain you feel is simply feelings of weakness being excreted from your being -- weakness doesn't go easily. It's just like lifting weights: you break down the muscles during your workout, and they rebuild themselves stronger so that that same workload does not break them down the next time. Emotional distress is not a signal to stop what you're doing -- pain is a call to action. What can I change? What can I be better at? Where did I make mistakes that can be corrected in the future?

Taking action is a choice when you feel pain. Make your choice.

Make Plans Bigger Than Yourself.

You need a reason to get up in the morning. You won't feel like getting up every day. There will be days when you feel like sleeping another hour, and no one would call you out for doing so. You could get away with it. This means that on some days we all need a reason to get up that is bigger than just being who we are and doing for ourselves. We need a purpose.

Do you want to crawl and drag yourself through a day when you get up, or would you rather be excited and jump from under the covers? The difference between the two is found in having a purpose for getting up, a purpose that drives you.

You get to that energy level by having a goal that is a lot bigger than the prospects of five more minutes of sleep. Set a goal for yourself that is just big enough that it's impossible without your full top-level effort. Lofty purposes require lofty amounts of energy and focus and commitment. If you feel yourself dragging through your days, with no real direction and nothing to be excited about, reevaluate your goals and relocate your purpose.

Haters & Naysayers.

When you notice people sending negative energy in your direction, congratulations. That means you're making something meaningful happen. If your work was worthless or not impactful, no one would care to give it attention, positive or negative. Nobodies do not attract negativity from observers simply because there is nothing to bring down in a nobody. Detractors target those who have something worthwhile to rail against. If you happen to be the target of a detractor, pat yourself on the back.

People who are actively against your cause are useful, based on simple physics: Energy is neither created nor destroyed -- it is merely transferred from one object to another. So their negative energy serves to help you, in whichever way you choose to bend it. Our human bodies take in oxygen, refine it, and use the resulting products to power our brains and muscles and internal organs. You can do the same with the negative energy from your naysayers. Use the negative energy sent your way and refine it -- make it into a useful form to be directed for your purposes. In this way, anything sent your way helps you. The people seeking to bring you down, in reality, are powering you up.

And remember to say "thank you!" to your helpers.

Are You Ready For Your Future Competition?

There is someone who has similar goals to you, working to be ready to beat you. You two don't even know each other exists. There is someone who knows who you are -- but you don't know who they are -- who is preparing to go against you one day. There is a person who is better than you currently, who knows and expects you to be gunning for him. And he is doing what he needs to do to be ready to defeat all challengers.

What are you getting ready for? Is your current competition not at the level of the opponents you envision facing in the future? Then there are changes you need to make. The challengers you'll face in the future will be better, in the future, than they are right now. This means you'll need to be better too, and what you're doing now will reflect in your future performance.

Is it enough?

Consistency Of Effort.

I've been on the basketball court with people who felt, that day, motivated to become better players. It may have been because they were having a great day playing, which encouraged them, or a terrible day on the court, which reminded them of the work left to do. They'd ask me if we could work out together. Most of the time, they'd show up for several days or even a couple weeks. But eventually they all disappeared.

In the moment, when the pain or elation is being felt, it's easy to commit, at least orally, to some long-term action (how many intimate relationships become "official" in between bed sheets)?. What makes the commitment real, though, is where you are on Day 54, Day 223, and Day 1,000.

Name one thing you've made it to Day 1,000 (roughly three consecutive years) of.

Anything?

Anything worth doing in life takes time and effort. If it were easy, everyone would have done it or be doing it, and the abundance of "I've done thats" alone diminishes its value. What makes the meaningful things in life meaningful is that they are unique to you -- no one else can feel them the way you feel or felt them. The most important things you'll accomplish in life, many will never come close to the experience you gained in doing them.

Effort takes time and energy, which means you cannot do it all, and do it well. Find out what your purpose is --

what you were meant to do with this life you've been given -- and focus your energy towards that purpose. Make your focused effort a habit and results must follow.

Think Of What You Have -- Not What You Don't Have.

A financially struggling married couple worked hard every day to provide for their children. Though there was never anything extra left over, there was always food on the table and their family was a happy one. One year the couple decided to finally do something special for their family: they would go on a cruise. The husband and wife saved their money all year and managed to have just enough to get the whole family on the cruise.

Finally on the cruise, the couple had no extra money to buy food or drinks during their vacation. They subsisted on water and watched helplessly as the other cruisers enjoyed endless food and imbibed from the wide selection of drinks.

On the last day of the cruise, the family walked by a couple sharing a succulent shrimp cocktail. The poor husband approached the eating couple while they ate.

He explained his family's situation to the diners, how they had spent every dime they had just to get on the cruise and had nothing left over to buy food. Please, the husband begged, just let us have a shrimp, just one. We'll split it five ways!

The man eating the shrimp looked at the husband and laughed incredulously. "Man," he said, "all the food on this cruise is free!"

The couple who had struggled and strived so hard just to get their family on the cruise had become so focused on what they didn't have -- extra money -- that they never noticed what was right in front of them: all the food and drink their bellies could hold. This happens to us in our every day lives all the time. We look at what other people have and compare it to what we have and wish we had more. We complain that our situation is not as easy as the next person's was. All the while we are ignoring what we have at our own disposal right in front of us, wasting what we have while wishing it were all different. There are many people who would be very happy to have what you have right now. Your health, your possessions, your environment, your family & friends. The resources around you are more than enough to get you where you want to go if you would just stop looking outside of yourself and utilize what you have, which is plenty.

Do You Believe You?

It feels good to have the support of friends, family and fans. It's great when there are people in our corner who believe in us and what we can do. But this can only hold you up for so long, or even exist at all, if you do not believe in yourself.

People don't line up to ride on a train that's not going anywhere. We follow momentum. And the best way to get momentum behind you is to create it yourself.

When you believe in you, your energy infects everyone you come in contact with and allows them -- gives them permission and an impetus -- to follow you and believe in you.

I receive email from individuals seeking direction. They describe their life situations to me, then ask me what the possibilities are for what they can do. How would I know what you are capable of? How will you ever know, if you don't believe in yourself enough to see what possibilities your life holds? You have to look in the mirror and ask yourself what is possible for your life, then take the actions to do it. No one can determine that for you and you should never let or ask anyone to take that power to decide your fate.

Nobody follows a person until that person makes it okay for themselves to be followed. This is not done with any particular words or grand gestures. Your belief is what draws that energy.

Whom do you believe in?

Bring A Competitive Mentality. You'll Need It.

The world we live in is competitive. Getting into to your preferred college is a competition amongst students. People who mow lawns for a living are competing to keep their customers. Supermarkets are competing to keep you shopping there. In everything you see going on around you, there is some entity trying to take something away or keep something from another entity that wants their spot.

Ignoring this dynamic or pretending that it doesn't exist won't make it go away and will likely cost you dearly in the long run as the wolves out there devour your stake. It doesn't mean you have to be a cutthroat savage about protecting your territory -- that works for some people but it doesn't have to be your method unless that is your personality -- but you must know that anything you do that is worth a damn will be challenged in many ways.

If you approach your business with your fists balled, figuratively speaking, paradoxically, fewer people will bother picking with you. What this means is, make it clear that you are ready to protect what's yours and will go down fighting to keep it. This mental state emanates from within, and affects everything you do. People can sense this without you uttering a word. It will not exempt you from needing to compete but there will be many who decide it better to leave you be than risk what would happen bothering you.

If you want to win, you'll have to compete -- with yourself first. The more you win, the more challenges will appear before you. Once you decide you no longer wish to stand your ground, and tire of the mental grind, you'll have two choices: step aside or be eaten alive.

Everything You Want, Wants You.

It's just waiting for you to come seize it or become it. Whomever you want to be, that Future You wants you to get there and become that person. That car you saw in the magazine is just waiting for you to come and sit in the driver's seat.

We discussed the power of energies. When your energy is directed towards a certain goal, that goal's energy responds in kind. As long as you can maintain focused, determined attention to this goal, you and your goal have no choice but to grow closer to each other.

Everything you're envisioning, is waiting for you to come and meet it halfway. All you need to do is take action and go get it.

Picking Yourself Up Mentally.

Our plans never go exactly as expected. Sometimes outcomes go in the complete opposite direction of our plans. We hope for the best, but the worst outcome sometimes results in life. It has happens to me, you, and anyone else who you know or can name.

Your challenge is to not allow those downturns to press you down mentally or cause you to lower your standards and expectations. Be like a rubber ball: the harder you're thrown down, the higher you bounce back up.

Your mind is your strongest ally, and can be your biggest enemy if you do not control it. When setbacks occur and you find yourself down mentally, your job is pick yourself up as quickly as you can -- train your mind to never stay down no matter what happens.

Confidence Is Everything.

Confidence is your own personal belief in what you can accomplish. You're confident you can tie your shoes or drive your car, because you've done it many times successfully with no problems.

So, someone may ask, how do I become confident in something that I've never accomplished? The answer is, 1) Do it, learn from your mistakes and develop the confidence, and 2) In the meantime until you become proficient, fake it.

Fake It?

Understand that we humans, by default, take most of what we see and hear at face value. Questioning everything presented to us every day takes more physical, mental and emotional energy than we have or care to expend. People will accept you for what you present yourself as, and maybe, if there is reason, dig deeper into you later. This is also true when dealing with ourselves: tell yourself about your confidence, make yourself feel that you are very confident in some task. You will be confident, because your mind doesn't discern between fantasy and reality. Put real belief behind that fantasy and it becomes very, very real.

First impressions last. So if you are approaching a task that you're new to and want to feel confident, pretend for that moment that you're not you: Become a person who, for whatever reason, would feel supreme confidence being in the position that you're in. Be that person. Walk like them. Talk like them. Think like them. Have the look in your eye that they would have.

Then go and do it.

Be Who You Are.

We already talked about how competitive the world is. Anything that you have going good for yourself, someone, somewhere along the line is going to go against you to grab a piece of it for themselves. But there is one area in life where no one can outdo you, no matter their resources, intelligence or life experience: Being you.

Being yourself is a one-man race that you cannot lose. The more you try to be someone or something you are not, the more you're running away from your most potent power. The power of fully being yourself cannot be copied or stolen from you by anyone else. No one can steal this idea and profit from it. It is a power which will lie dormant until you, and only you, take full advantage of it.

We all turn our heads and pay attention when something new comes along. When you fully and truly express who you are as a person, eventually the world embraces it because it has never been seen before and will never be seen again. That is your power.

As author Frank Ghery said, you may not be the best at expressing who you are, but you are the world's one and only expert in the subject.

You can't lose.

Practice Your Belief.

The practice of having complete and total belief in yourself is like the results of lifting weights: you practice on a consistent program, increasing your effort and output in small increments. You begin to focus on the work because you know results will not come overnight. Then one day you look in the mirror and the muscles are there.

Belief is the fuel behind everything you'll do today -- driving your car, brushing your teeth, walking up stairs. You can do those things because of your inherent belief that you can -- so strong that you never have to think about it.

For the more challenging tasks, you may need more time and practice. This is where belief comes from: just an ounce of courage to try something for the first time, creates something to be built on for the next time. Every self-believing person had to start with something, a small step on faith to just try. You must do the same. Once you prove to yourself that that one step was not so bad, the next, bigger step is easier. Then you can take a leap. This applies to anything you want to do in life.

Practice having the feeling of knowing you can do anything you set out to do -- just taking that small step over and over, every time. This practice crystallizes into a habit, and these habits become your character.

When you believe in yourself people can feel it emanating from you, in turn increasing their belief levels in you, just by being in your presence. Believe that you can be that person. Just take the small step of increasing your belief right now and see what a difference it makes.

Don't Seek Approval.

Humans are creatures of habit. We like things that are predictable and we like to reference any new idea against the ideas and beliefs we already accept and agree with.

So when something totally new, without precedent, comes along, our natural impulse is to resist, because this new thing represents a shakeup to our normal mental or physical routines. We are naturally resistant to change. So if you want to share something you made that has no precedent to reference, resistance should be expected. Enough resistance, even just one negating word, sometimes, to some people is outright and total rejection. Rejection causes some people to pack up and leave. In other words, to quit.

Seeking approval of yourself or your creations from others is not the fast track to acceptance. If you are being who you are or what you're presenting is coming from deep within you, that in itself is the approval. Like we talked about in the belief chapter, when you've approved of yourself, everyone else has no choice but to follow suit.

As Long As Your Mind Still Sees It, It's Possible.

Life is full of long, tough journeys. The toughest will take years and will show you many setbacks and dark days. This is a part of the process. There will be many times when you look up and the physical manifestation of what you want to accomplish is nowhere to be seen. This is the point where many people opt of the game and quit, because success does not seem reachable. No one would fault you for feeling like quitting at one of these points.

Physically, there's a lot that we can't see. When you drive out of your job or school parking lot you can't see your house, but you keep driving because you know it's there, mentally, and you know you can get there, physically. Traveling in heavy rain or snow or fog, it's hard to see much further ahead of your headlights but we move forward because we know there's pavement to walk or drive on if we just keep going, and we know our destination isn't moving from where it is.

As long as you can still see the You that you aim to become, or the creation that you aim to create, in your mind, you can still get there. Your vision of who or what you wish to become is the most valuable asset you own. Nurture it, protect it, be willing to fight for it.

When you cease to see your vision in your mind, that's when it's over.

Crush Your Opposition.

Our world is competitive. People want what you have and they will not hesitate to take you out when the opportunity presents itself. This fact is not limited to sports or vocations in which overt aggression is applauded. If you wear a suit & tie to work, there are adversaries coming for your neck; they wear smiles on their faces, which makes recognizing them more difficult for you than say, a running back recognizing an opposing middle linebacker in football.

This information is not shared to turn you into a bloodthirsty savage (unless that's your sort of thing). It's about knowing that some of the people you're in competition with are bloodthirsty savages and they want your head (figuratively speaking, I hope). Practical reasoning says that you need to arm yourself to play the game that you're in.

When you compete, aim to win in a manner that eliminates your opponent from ever being a threat to you again. Make them think it better to find a new foil to tangle with next time rather than face the consequences of squaring off against you and your team. Take away their will to compete with you.

As the 90's video game Mortal Kombat used to say, "Finish Him!"

Don't Worry About What Anyone Else Is Doing.

Facebook, Twitter, other social media and the blogosphere have created an entire universe where you can spend hours upon hours reading and writing and opining about what other people are doing, have done or are about to do.

If you are aiming to get ahead and not just get by in your pursuits, set aside dedicated time to get off of the time-wasting treadmill and focus on you and what you need to get done. It sounds very simple but you would be surprised to see how many people rarely do this apart from the time they are being supervised to do dedicated work. The more you focus on you, naturally, the more you'll get out of yourself. When you're focused on you, you'll realize how much time you were wasting that you can now redirect to getting stuff done.

What you'll find is, the more time you spend focusing on what you're doing and not anyone else, you may start to become the person who the time-wasters talk about.

Find Inspiring Influences.

Your inspiration won't and doesn't have to always come from within (though it helps to be self-sufficient in this way -- it can be always counted on). We know that motivation and inspiration must be constantly renewed, just like we consistently take showers and baths. You can save yourself a lot of time and energy by taking advantage of your resources: Using the things in your environment for inspiration.

Use the resources at your disposal: listen to and observe other people. Watch videos. Read literature. Listen to music. Find anything which speaks to your soul and allows that energy to seep into you. Keep it handy -- on your phone, a picture near your bathroom mirror, a reminder in your gym bag. The more, the better and the more often, the more effective.

Value Your Time.

It's all you really have in this life. Any material possession -- money, clothes, your car -- can be taken away from you just as easily as it is acquired. Time is the great equalizer. Though we all have a different total amount of it on earth, while here we're all equal: 24 hours per day. Being taller or richer or a certain nationality or religion cannot buy you more time and nothing you do or say will change the fact that you have to live through 24 hours every single day you're alive.

Each one of us has a fixed amount of time to be alive on this earth and then it's over. Whatever you choose to do with that time, that daily 24 hours, that's all that will be left to represent your time here when you're gone.

Waste enough minutes and they become hours. Wasted hours turn to days. Wasted days, weeks and months add up faster than you think and you'll wake up one day wondering what the hell happened to your life.

With the mindset that time is the only thing you really own in this world, you'll find yourself doing less of the wasteful activities that get you no closer to the life and achievements you want. Fewer wasteful, useless people in your circle. Fewer useless thoughts and actions. Every minute counts, literally -- it's counting right now.

Don't waste yours.

Appreciate Yourself.

To get where you are going in life, many people will be involved from time to time. You'll receive some help from someone, or many someones, somewhere along the way. In the long run, though, any place worth getting to will require much more of your own personal efforts than anyone else's. If you're going to reach your lofty goals, you will be doing much more of the work, on your own, than anyone else can possibly help you with.

Most of us are great at depreciating ourselves. We make false shows of modesty when people talk us up to others. We constantly compare ourselves to others, and since there will always be someone better or with more, we voluntarily generate feelings of inferiority. Why not go the other way and truly appreciate ourselves for who we are? After all, you are the one doing all the work. You are grinding through those rough days. We cannot control outcomes but we can control effort. Consistent effort is not easy.

For this effort, find time to appreciate yourself. You saw the vision before anyone else did. You did the legwork and suffered through those setbacks and dark days. You deserve a pat on the back and there's no reason for you to wait for someone to give it to you.

Give it to yourself.

Focus on What You Can Control.

Many things will happen in your life that you can't do a damn thing about. People make decisions and do things which you cannot influence. Even times when you feel you do have some influence over a situation, others can behave unpredictably. No matter how hard you try, you cannot control everything in life. The harder you try to control everything, the harder things become.

Your power will come from focusing on the things you can control, most importantly your attitude and your effort. You control your responses to life's events, which will inevitably include unpredictable twists and turns. No matter what happens, no matter what is thrown at you, you always have 100% control over your attitude. What you'll find is, your control over your attitude will increase the amount of control you have over events. The more you direct your focus towards what you can control, you'll find your circle of influence -- the things you *can* affect -- expanding.

We know that the things we focus our energy on increases those things. The more you focus on things within your circle of influence, the wider that circle grows. Paradoxically, if you put mental energy into the things you cannot control, you'll find more things that you cannot control coming to your attention. This is how our minds work -- anything you focus on creates more of it.

Focus on your influence.

Fundamentals First.

Every endeavor has its basics, the building blocks. Basketball players must learn to make layups. Lawyers must know how to prepare briefs. Leaders learn how to motivate and influence others. Drug dealers learn how to package their products for sale on the street.

The process of learning the fundamentals is boring and monotonous. Reality TV shows don't get made about the fundamentals of any vocation because the basics of most our work is neither exciting nor glamorous. But, if you want to build something that does draw the attention of the masses (or even a small crowd to start out with), start with the basics.

Think of it like building a high-rise condominium or office building. If the foundation -- the base ground floor which will support everything else -- is weak, the first strong rainstorm or heavy winds will send your 80-story creation tumbling down along with everything in it. Having a luxurious, fancy top floor is only as valuable as the amount of care and detail that was put into making sure the base level was strong enough to hold everything built upon it. Don't short yourself on the basics unless you're willing and able to pay three times as much later on down the line. And we already know there isn't any time to waste.

Bad Or Good: Whatever You Make It.

We've discussed attitude, how the way you look at things -- which is completely your choice -- will shape your life.

Every event, no matter how it looks on the surface, has a hidden advantage, an opportunity, within it. Train yourself to look at all the events in your life in this manner and you'll start finding these opportunities more often.

How do you do this? Any time something happens, ask yourself, What is the advantage of this circumstance? What can I do with this situation that advances my position? How can I turn these circumstances in a direction that fuels my momentum? This frame of mind -- asking yourself a different set of questions -- challenges you to find the useful material in every situation. Your brain absolutely has the power to do this; this power is laying dormant within you.

"Bad" and "Good" are definitions we made up, serving to define every event in our lives. We want to assign a label to every circumstance before digging deep into it. What we must understand is that no situation is bad or good; every event in life is neutral. Our mental response frames it as good or bad. With this new frame of mind -- everything neutral -- ask yourself, What can be gained from this? What can be learned?

Bad and good are under your control. Use them and your new way of thinking to your advantage.

Get Advice Only From Those Who Have Done It.

"Everybody can tell you how to do it, they never did it." - Jay-Z

When you're on a path towards an accomplishment, there will be much unsolicited advice thrown your way for free. The anonymity of Internet commentating has multiplied this force. Most of this unsolicited advice will come from those who have not done what you're looking to do, or even as much as taken the first step to get where you're currently at, much less where you're going.

You're unique and your situation is, down in the details, completely unique. No one has ever had your exact circumstances before and no one will ever again. If you're going to listen to some advice, take it from a person who is where you want to be, who has traveled the road you are facing. Even though they will never have your exact circumstance, they know the path better than anyone. They have an understanding of where you're at and where you are trying to go.

Commenting from the peanut gallery is cheap, fast and easy. There is no entry cost and the products of the peanut gallery are equally worthless. Usually in life the people who have done things rarely do that much talking about those things, compared to those who haven't. Those who have done things feel no need to talk so much -- when you've done something the need to talk about it diminishes greatly.

If you want useful advice, seek out the accomplished. These people may not be easy to find -- remember they likely aren't boasting much -- and are often busy because accomplishments beget accomplishments: They are on to the next thing. Their time is valuable and there may not be much of it offered to you. The less there is of something, the more value it has -- the Law of Scarcity.

The fast, cheap and easy opinions from the peanut gallery? Not worth the time you spend taking it in.

You Are Either Building or Destroying.

Every thought you have, every little itty-bitty move you make, is either building or destroying your future, your environment, your team, your relationships. There are no neutral actions in this world.

Stop right now and ask yourself, what were you just thinking? Was that thought building you up for the future or was it destroying you? In simpler terms, is it helping or hurting you? Same question for the last action you took. Is that action making you better or worse?

A house gets built one brick at a time. Every brick in your personal house either strengthens your house's foundation or makes it easier for the Big Bad Wolf (setbacks, bad days, unexpected events, the unpredictable actions of others) to blow your house down. The great thing about your personal house is, you can replace weak bricks with strong bricks without having to tear the entire edifice down. Enough weak bricks needing replacement will keep you from ever adding size to your house (in the form of more accomplishments, influence, knowledge), as you're constantly working on fixing the broken parts rather than building anew.

You are the head contractor building the house of your life. So start adding strong bricks to your house right now so it is ready for the inevitable storms of life.

If You're Really Working It Will Show.

When you're focused and doing the work there's not much you need to say. Good work is self-evident -- don't mess it up by adding to the conversation. Shut up and get to work.

Put in enough solid work and others will begin to do the speaking for you. We humans are alike in many ways, one way being that we talk about people who are making things happen. You have, in the last week, spent some time thinking or talking about someone you hardly know and who hardly knows you, because of whatever that person is doing and the effect is has on you. When you dig deep into your work and stay focused, you become the topic of those conversations.

When people are talking about your work, no matter whet they're saying, it draws more attention to your work. So do the work, then let that work do all the work of publicizing you and starting conversations.

Recognize Your Calling.

Everything ain't for everybody. We all will try many things in life, but there is a specific task that you were meant for. You may be spending the majority of your time doing things that are not even close to that task.

This meant-for-you task cannot be prescribed to you by anyone else. This task speaks to your inner being when you're doing it, and you can feel it. Problem is, many of us repeatedly ignore this calling and force ourselves into some task that is not for us.

There are many reasons this happens -- outside pressure, keeping up appearances, eagerness to satisfy others. This leads to weakened energy and utter frustration with our lives because we continuously ignore or resist the call coming from where we really belong.

Sit alone and really think deeply: Where am I meant to be? Only you can answer this; You know you better than anyone else does, and no one can tell you how you feel when you are doing things.

What task or activity, when you're immersed in it, really speaks to your inner-self? What work could you do for hours or days without looking at the clock? What business would you gladly work in for free?

This is where you belong. And you will find a way to get there.

5 Keys: Work. Focus. Study. Stick To It. Believe.

Practice and put in the time to master the necessary skills. There is no substitute for hard work. Heed this advice or try, futilely, to prove it untrue -- it's been tried.

Block out distractions and put all of your mental & physical energy into the task. What we focus on increases; what we ignore diminishes.

Know your craft inside and out. See what is working and not working for others (also what worked and didn't work in the past) and how it may apply to your situation. Always know what's going on in your field of work. The information at our fingertips today makes this very easy to do in theory, but more challenging in practice because of the vigilance necessary to stay on top of things.

You can't fail until you quit. Losing is temporary and losing is something that happens to you; failure is a choice. By just showing up every day for as long as it takes, you'll outlast 90% of your peers on endurance alone, no matter your skill or talent level.

Nobody is going to follow, support, or believe in you wholeheartedly until you do. Once you believe you, everyone else has permission to follow.

Be Willing To Stand Alone.

There is plenty of room at the top, and it's lonely up there. Not all the people around you when you start out on your journey will be there at the end, if you manage to make it to the end. It is your job to make sure you are there.

As time goes on, your friends will begin showing up less often -- persistence is boring and most people cannot stand being bored. There will be many days when you're alone. What are you gonna do? Stay there and do your work alone, continuing to show up, or will you fall by the wayside like all the rest did, joining them in the next new and exciting activity (which you'll be leaving, too, when it gets boring)? The answer to that question will determine your success level.

Look at the most successful people you know; if you can, talk to them. You will find that they do many things -- most importantly their work -- alone. The spoils of their success draws an audience. There is much unglamorous time in their schedule, and no one is, or wants to be, around for that. But they get it done, and that is the key to their success.

Have A Bad Memory.

The human mind is a dutiful servant. I'll show you.

Ask your brain, right now, to deliver some positive response that uplifts you and makes you feel good about yourself. Tell your brain to tell you why you are attractive and desirable to the opposite sex. Tell your brain to deliver, along with these thoughts, some actual examples from your life to back up this thinking. Your brain will, immediately, do as you told it to.

Now, tell your mind to bring up that time when you messed up, when you were the worst out of everyone, and felt like you were completely failing at life. Remember that time when you just wanted to dig a hole and bury yourself in it so no one could see you. See what happens? Those thoughts were delivered, right on time, and brought you right back to those inferior feelings. Each and every time, your mind delivers whatever you order.

Your mind is like a Pizza Hut delivery person on steroids -- always bringing exactly what you want, on time, hot and fresh to your door. Never closed for business, never a busy signal, never asking you to hold due to other customers. Whatever you choose to store in your memory, your mind will have it hot and ready to deliver to your conscious train of thought as soon as the call -- your conscious thought -- comes in.

Have a bad memory when it comes to negative, useless and energy-draining thoughts and feelings. Treat those negative thoughts and ideas like rotten pepperoni or bad cheese and dispose of them when you're aware of their existence. They will not be on your pizza.

Keep bad ingredients out of your kitchen and they can never end up in your food.

Outside Motivation Only Goes So Far. Is It In You?

That includes this book. All the videos and literature in the world cannot make you want to go put in the long-term hard work necessary to reach the level of precision you'll need to reach the top level of any endeavor (at least not in the long run). Any motivational tool can get you started -- like jumper cables on a car -- but to sustain that momentum your car is going to depend on its own   battery and it will need some gas: Your self-generated motivation.

It has to be in you. You're not going to want to practice every day. You won't want to read that last chapter of text when you're studying on a Friday night. The only thing left to push you towards that final effort is your ability to pull it out of you. That "it" has to be in there, however, in order for it to be pulled out. The best way to motivate yourself is simple: find something to do that you don't need to constantly look for motivation to be doing. Any chosen task should move you on its own. If it doesn't, turn and go in a different direction.

When doing something that you have to do but may not necessarily want to be doing, a little bit of mental dexterity does the trick: Find the underlying necessity of the task that does move you. For example, if you're studying for a chemistry test, the fact that a high grade on the test will get you a 'B' mark in chemistry class which will make you eligible to play sports the following year in college. That can be your driving thought.

The human brain is the most powerful tool known to man. Tap into yours in ways you may not have before and exploit its powers.

Check Yourself.

We all have our own running internal dialogue that speaks to us about what we do, what we see, and how we feel about it. That dialogue, since it's ours, tends to skew towards telling us what we want to hear most of the time, if it goes unchecked. Sometimes you need to get out of your head and really listen to what you're telling yourself.

Make a habit of stepping back and looking at your actions as if they were the actions of another person. What would you think of this person? Considering their actions alone, what would you think this person is looking to do with their life? Does this person's actions align with their words?

Be responsible for checking yourself from time to time. What are you pretending not to see? What lies are you feeding yourself to make yourself feel better? Analyze your actions and decide, honestly, if those actions line up with where you plan to go in your life. Adjust if necessary.

Use What You've Got.

If you look around enough, you'll see that there is always someone with more, with better. There will always be someone whose circumstances seem to be much more favorable than yours. If we're not careful we can get bogged down into the type of what-if thinking that is always asking how different things would be if we only had more, if we had it just as easy as the next person does. This I-Wish mindset immobilizes you as you let it sink in, and you start to buy into just how hard life is for poor little you.

This type of thinking is completely unproductive and useless because it creates a cycle of built-in excuses. All that you have at your disposal, right now, is all you need to get the job done. There are people who have made more out of less than what you have now, so there are no excuses. When you set your mind to make the most of whatever is at your disposal, you are already on the offensive. When go do it, it becomes a habit and an expectation you have for yourself.

You use resources, but you are not at the mercy of your resources. Everything in front of you, no matter how much or how little, is a tool and you make the most of what you have. Your self is your most potent and versatile weapon; everything else is a nice accessory that can be replaced or compensated for.

Take Care of Business.

This is most important concerning tasks that you alone are responsible for with no one watching over you or double-checking on your progress.

When we work at jobs and have a boss, the work gets done because that work gets inspected. If it is not done, our supervisors will know immediately and the punishments are just as immediate. When you are working on your own volition only you are responsible for handling your business. If you choose to waste time and nothing gets done, no one will know or care. No one is checking on it and no one can crack the whip to make you work.

What does get you moving in this situation, is what we call "self-discipline." The Business of You runs on your energy. If you slack off, your business slacks off. If you're focused on getting things done, The Business of You will be get things done.

Be An Opportunist: Embrace and Make the Most of Your Situation.

We have discussed how there is opportunity all around you, when you've adjusted your mindset to look for the usefulness of every situation.

The term "opportunist" -- "a person who exploits circumstances to gain immediate advantage rather than being guided by consistent principles or plans" -- has negative connotations in our society. We generally think of an opportunist as a person who is always looking to take advantage, even to the detriment of others. But the word simply defines one who is seeking opportunity, creates opportunity, and acts quickly to capitalize on opportunity. Don't we all want to be that?

When circumstances are favorable an opportunist does not kick her feet up and relax. She seeks ways to build on it and keep the momentum going. The most dire of circumstances contains a hidden gem of opportunity to the trained eye, to the opportunist. Having less puts you in position to be resourceful and do more with less. A loss is a wake-up call which forces you to take a hard look at what you can do better and differently, now. Having friends or partners let you down or not do as expected is a chance to see just how much you can handle on your own.

There is opportunity in everything.

The opportunist does not let good times make their mind go soft and doesn't allow tough times to drive them to inaction. Everything is a tool to the resourceful craftsman.

Be Your Own #1 Fan.

No one likes to be the first person to a party -- you're alone and bored and there's no one to dance with or talk to. It's the same with creating a following for yourself. You must be the one to break the ice and get people up off of the walls and into the middle of the dance floor. Once you make it cool to support and be excited about you, other people will see that and know its OK for them to do it too. But you must take the lead, by being the first on the dance floor.

Don't be bashful about making your accomplishments known -- it's not bragging, it's reporting. Be proud of yourself and show it while demonstrating to others how they can join the party too, by supporting you. Being the first one out on the floor takes both courage and a bold spirit, and the bold and courageous person is quietly admired for his audacity (though few will ever express this to you). Being self-conscious and being bold, which is outwardly focused energy, do not go together. Being bold is a necessary trait to starting a movement.

Make your choices on who you will be.

You deserve recognition for your work, so be the first to announce and make it known. Others will follow your lead.

Relax Your Mind. (Meditation)

There's a lot going on in our days and we move around a lot. Between television, human interaction and our cell phones, we have a way to be mentally occupied for 24 hours a day if we so choose. However, the human brain is like your computer in that it works most efficiently and clean when it gets a "reboot" every now and then. For our computers we hit the restart button or turn the machine off for a while. For our minds, taking a few minutes out for meditation or just relaxing and letting go of our conscious train of thought -- intentionally thinking about nothing -- gets the job done.

There is no how-to procedure to follow for meditating, just some basic principles. Find a calm, relaxing environment where you will not be bothered for the amount of time you'll relax (can be thirty seconds, five minutes, a half hour, or no set time at all -- whatever you wish to begin with). Empty your mind and don't think about anything for this time (biggest challenge, which you will fail at repeatedly). Thoughts will come and go, so let them -- "see" the thoughts walking by, as author Russell Simmons says, and let them keep on walking. You can get back to them when you're done.

Whatever amount of time you can meditate, commit to an amount that's duplicable. That is, an amount you can do consistently. Make meditation a habit just like your job or your gym time is (not easy to do, I know this first hand) and reap the benefits of your consistent mental "re-start" to clear your head.

Life is Short. Do It Now.

We each have a finite amount of time on this earth and we all know that. That time, often, seems so distant and abstract amidst life's daily grind that we lose sight of the fact that ours could end at any moment.

When does yours end? How much life do you have left before it is taken from you?

If you're like me, you have no idea if you'll be here even a year from now. So that "someday" you speak of -- are you sure you're going to be around for it? Are you 100% sure that time is going to wait for you to do what you want to do in your short time here?

You don't have time to waste.

We willfully waste time in our lives with useless conversation and activities, busy work that is neither urgent nor important, worrying about a future that we may not even live to see. The only thing we truly have and can count on is the present moment. Right now is the only time we have and the only place in which we can do or affect anything. There is a project you want to start on or conversation you want to have that you are putting off until... When? When will the time be right for it, and how can you be sure? You and I both know you can't be sure that "someday" will work out as perfectly as we hope.

Better start doing the things you want to do, and do them as if your time is limited, because it is, even more than you think.

Better to Do It Than Not Do It.

Every life will have regrets. There will be situations we look back on and wish things had worked out differently. Dealing with regrets and putting them behind us is the height of the wisdom that comes with age and experience.

In my life, though, 99% of all regrets I can recall are regrets of things I *did not do* or something I did not say. There are very few things I have *done* which I wish I hadn't done at all, because even ill-advised actions leave the residue of learning experiences and stories to tell and knowledge gained.

Not doing something when you have the chance leaves... Nothing. Just empty thoughts of what could have been and a permanent what-if feeling eating away at you from within. Could-have-beens are the lost chances that you'll be kicking yourself about for the rest of your life. Ask anyone older than you and they will tell you the same.

Do something, and take the risk of being mad that you did it. The feeling of not knowing what could have happened is the worst feeling to have to live with.

Nothing ventured, nothing gained.

Keep Positive Reminders Around You.

You've done many great things in your life. You have accomplishments you're proud of, things you have been recognized for. There are moments in your life that bring up positive memories and energy. Wouldn't you like to have that energy at your fingertips? Well, why don't you?

Keep reminders in your environment, in whatever form you like, that will remind you of that positive energy and those great experiences. Pictures, music, items, people. Just like you push away and dispose of the negative reminders, seek and preserve the positive reminders and things that conjure those feelings up.

You will not feel 100% great every day of life, so cheat a little bit: use reminders like you would vitamins to boost yourself up when you need it. Your memories are your personal possession; use them to your advantage.

Where's Your Energy Going?

A law of physics: Energy is neither created nor destroyed; it is merely passed from one object to another.

Energy can be leaving you or accruing to you based on your thoughts, words and actions. Sharing your energy with others doesn't deplete yours; sharing energy causes it to multiply, we call this synergy.

The direction of your energy is important because whatever you send out, returns to you just like a mirror reflects back whatever is placed in front of it. Send your energy towards negative influences, you get the same sent back to you. Using your energy on positivity reflects positivity your way. We've discussed several times how your focus magnifies its target. The direction of your energy increases whatever you're using it on or for.

Similarly, however you decide to feel, or tell yourself how you feel, your energy will respond in kind. If you tell yourself that you're tired and listless and need rest, you energy levels will follow your directions and decrease. If you tell yourself that you feel great (try yelling this out while raising your arms in victory -- silly, but it really works) and you are ready for anything, your energy will rise in kind even on your longest days.

Energy is a very powerful force that more than makes up for what you lack in physical ability and knowledge if used properly. Aim yours in the right direction.

You Only Need To Be Right Once.

The title is a line made famous, to me at least, by Dallas Mavericks owner Mark Cuban. Mark was discussing business when he said this and it applies to whatever you do in your life. We all dabble in and try many things over time, but one area of high, intense concentration is all we need to find fulfillment.

There are many choices and directions for you to take in life. There are plenty of ways for you to be successful. You only need to choose one to put your energy into.

To become truly great in some pursuit, your complete focus is required. You put all your energy into mastering an area and separate yourself from the masses who only do things for fun (or when it's convenient or as long as there is no pain). Over a period of time, that focus helps you pull away in the race.

Partial focus leads to partial results. Only the foolish man thinks he can do everything which he sees others doing. Intensity defeats extension any time. Commit to being great at one thing, focus on it, and it will pay off.

Be The Boss of Your Organization.

Every organization, even those composed of just one person, needs a boss, someone in charge. You have bosses on your sports teams (your coach), at your school (teachers or principals) and at your job (managers, supervisors).

Who's the boss of the work you do when you're alone, the work you do for yourself?

If you plan to reach high levels of success, the Organization Of You needs a boss and you are the only candidate. You have the job, whether you want it or not. This means you hold yourself accountable for showing up on time, doing the necessary tasks properly, bringing the right effort, energy, and consistency.

In daily life, your teachers, supervisors and coaches make sure things get done correctly. You know that if you half-ass a job they will be there to call you out and make you do it right (or get rid of you). You, as the boss of the Organization Of You, have the responsibility of holding yourself accountable. No boss will let you show up 15 minutes late every day of work. No boss will ignore a weak effort right in front of her face. You would never offer 'I didn't feel like it' as an explanation to your boss; why accept it from yourself?

If you want to be taken seriously, take yourself seriously.

Greatness Makes No Excuses.

Think of the best performers   in the fields you pay attention to. Even though you may not know them personally, maybe you have some insight into the inner workings of the things they do through social media, television, books and magazines, etc. Study their habits, especially when things don't go as planned for them.

When things aren't going great for the top-level performers, there's no complaining. They don't blame their coworkers or teammates. There are no excuses to make. The best performers assume leadership roles, which means everyone is following their example. Sometimes they speak out but this is always preceded or followed by action -- we all know that actions speak louder than words.

If the leader complains or loses composure, the door is open for everyone else to complain. Winning organizations don't spend time complaining. They follow the example of their leader -- adjust, come right back and get the job done.

If you're going to be great, the best there is, what can you afford   to make excuses or complain about? Excuses are monuments to nothingness. But if you're reaching for greatness, and are uncompromising about it, no explanation is necessary.

Give Yourself Permission To Fail.

The fear of failure is responsible for more failings in individuals than any actual lack of ability or even the actual act of coming up short. Often we are so afraid of failing that we don't even make an attempt, and when we do try, we do not push ourselves to levels we could easily reach because we fear the consequences of aiming or climbing too high.

If you have ever experienced the fear of failure during a performance, you know how debilitating this handicap can be. You are tense and tight. Nervousness keeps you from loosening up, mentally and physically, you're cautious and averse to any form of risk. The existence of a fear of failure, is already failure for a performer. And observers can see this in you.

Flip this dynamic around: Give yourself permission to fail. Allow yourself to mess up and you'll come to realize that it is not nearly as bad as it seems, and you'll stop allowing fear to take over your mind.

Getting better at something inherently involves failure -- you will not be perfect at a new, challenging skill the first or even the fifth time. In a competitive environment you'll be facing opponents just as good as you are, and no one is perfect every day or every game. You will suffer defeats. A person who has never failed at anything has never tried anything worth doing. The great achievers in life fail their way to the top of their fields, learning from each attempt and coming back even stronger. Allowing yourself to fail is, paradoxically, allowing yourself the room to succeed.

So start failing now.

Easy Success Tip: Show Up.

Persistence and perseverance are skills. A person who can show up and put forth a consistent effort longer than everyone else is a special person. Want to make yourself invaluable? Be that person. You'll be relied upon because the people around you will know what to expect from you: You'll be there, on time, every time, ready to go.

If you want more luck, you have to invite luck into your life. How is this done? First, we need to know what luck is: The meeting of preparation and opportunity. How do you get prepared? By doing the work. Where is opportunity found? In front of any person who is active and alert and open to the possibilities of life.

If you bury yourself into your own mind and close off your thinking, luck cannot find you. If you want some luck, show up where you'd like to meet it and open your mind to the opportunities around you. Luck follows no schedule, so luck may not be there the first or even the fourth time -- this is the point at which those who are depending solely on luck to do their work will quit.

Want to be different? Want to stand out? Want to last?

Then keep showing up.

Defeat The Negativity.

You've had this experience. Something happens that sprouts a negative thought in your head. For whatever reason, you entertain this thought (STOP doing this!) and your brain then goes to work, delivering increasingly negative thoughts to support your original thought. Before you know it, you're mentally down about a hypothetical situation that may never even happen, or down about the worst possible interpretation of some aspect of your life.

Negative thoughts roll downhill this way -- once they're around you and you let them into your conscious mind, they gain momentum and each thought builds on the next.

Treat any negative thought that tries to take root in your mental garden just like a weed -- grab it by the throat, yank it out of the ground and kill it, never to be seen again. Weeds thrive when they go unchecked and can feed off of the fertile ground of our minds.

Tend to your garden, and be ready to protect it at all times.

Who's Around You, Who Wants You Around?

A wise man once said, "Go where you're adored, not where you're ignored."

Think of the people, the places, the activities that make you feel good, where positive results are produced, where your positive energy flows outward and it is returned to you. Think, how can I spend more of my time in these environments?

Now think of the energy drainers, the people and places that seem to drain your energy and psyche. How do you feel when you know you're soon to be around these people and places? Why are you around there? Is there something forcing you to be around them which you cannot control? If not, why not make changes? If so, how can you use your resources to alter the environment? This is your life, after all. Every minute could be your last.

Think of the people who are happy to have you in their circle -- they always ask why you're not around more often. When you leave, they want to know when you're coming back. You're greeted with smiles and general positivity that you can feel. These are the places that you need to be spending your time and energy. How often are you in these environments -- once in a blue moon or is this part of your regular schedule?

Where are you adored, where are you ignored? Adjust where and how you spend your time to be around energy which builds you up.

Walk Away in Strength, Not Weakness.

Not everything you get involved in will end with the results you want. So, sometimes it's smart to cut your losses and walk away. When you do, do it from a position where you're walking away because you want to: You've put in your full effort and decided to go in another direction. You have no regrets. You're not walking away in weakness, where you left opportunities on the table and came up short because you were never fully committed.

Walking away in strength is when you've put in your best effort, have decided to pivot, and know you can do better at your next destination. On the other hand when walking away in weakness, you feel like you lost something before you got to make use of it. Walking away in strength leaves you feeling empowered. It's like sitting down to eat a dinner you prepared yourself after a full, honest day's work. Every day, good or bad, always ends, and in life there are things we need to move on from. When it comes time, be satisfied with your efforts and move on.

What You Think, Attracts More of It.

Every thought your mind has produces a wave of energy that is magnetic -- it attracts its own frequency and brings more of that energy back to you. Thoughts beget words which produce actions and repeated actions form habits. Those habits create your character and in turn, virtue.

Think of a time you had a flow of positive thoughts in your mind -- they come in bunches -- and you allowed a negative, defeating thought a seat at your positive-thought table. If it did not immediately extinguish your positive flow, this negative thought invited some of its negative-thought friends, and quickly took over the space.

Positive-thought flow, gone.

Next time you're feeling not-so-great about a situation, take a break from it and think of some reasons you have to feel good -- your family, health, something fun you did last week. Better yet, next time you're in the midst of having a great time somewhere, revisit a challenging situation you've been dealing with -- with a mindset of taking constructive action towards fixing it -- and you'll be amazed how much the clouds have cleared from above it.

Be Real With Yourself.

We keep running narratives in our heads of every situation in our lives to keep up with everything that's happening. These stories we're telling ourselves may or may not reflect reality; we skew the truth (in our heads) from time to time keep ourselves sane and sheltered from the cold, harsh realities staring us in the face. To keep our minds at ease we rationalize. Everyone does it, whether it be to justify a dubious action, give ourselves courage to act or speak up on a situation, or ease our conscious minds so we can relax and go to sleep at night.

When it comes to the most important of matters (at least at the beginning, then we can work out way backwards to even the slightest trifles), it's important that you look at everything in as clear and realistic a light as possible. That means being real with and about yourself -- your strengths and weaknesses, opportunities and threats, as well as those of others around you whom you need to deal with every day.

To get a clear analysis of yourself and your situations you must see what is really there, no matter how uncomfortable that reality may be. This requires turning off that constant internal dialogue in your head and seeing everything for what it really is. Again, this reality could be unpleasant, but seeing everything in a clear light of reality is incredibly liberating and will open possibilities to you as you turn this practice into habit.

When you tell yourself lies your life becomes a lie, inauthentic and fabricated.

Someone Above You Is Doing Something You're Not Doing.

If another person is in the same field of work as you, and they're doing better or accomplishing more than you, there's something they are doing, or have done, in their everyday lives that you're not doing. Your job -- if you want to have their spot -- is to change that equation.

Read and inform yourself about your work and what is going on in your field that may affect or be affecting you.

Ask questions about yourself and about those who are ahead of you. Talk to those who know you and ask them what they think of your work (this person need not be an expert in, or even involved in your field. The observations of a casual observer can prove quite clairvoyant if you know what to listen for).

Step outside of yourself and imagine that you're watching you, doing the things you do. What would you think of that person? If you didn't know them, what would you say this person is moving towards? What's important to them? What is this person about? What's missing from what they do now, to get this person to where this person claims they want to go? Do their actions align with their stated goals? Why or why not?

Find out what you're missing. Then go and get it.

No One Can "Make You Feel" Anything.

We've discussed how thoughts lead to words and words to actions. So by controlling your thoughts you have control over the way you feel and the things you do. What another person says or does, does not force you to feel any particular way, so resolve to stop giving away this power to other people.

You have full choice over how you respond to external stimuli. Nothing can make you feel any type of way. You messed up terribly in front of a lot of people. Who says you have to feel terrible about it for even one second? Embarrassment is not something that happens to you; embarrassment is a state of mind. Your state of mind is a choice. The exact same thing can happen to two different people and their reactions can be completely different -- because each has full choice over their response.

How you feel is always 100% your choice and 100% within your power. Are you using it?

If another person says something negative or something meant to demean you, you can choose to allow those words to bring you down. You can choose to deny those words the power to have any effect on you, taking that power for yourself and taking full control over your feelings. Allowing the opinions of others to control how you feel about yourself is an uncomfortable and unpredictable roller coaster ride. You're up and down, hot and cold, based on every word sent your way. We know we cannot control another person's words.

Knowing this, would you choose to let your emotions live on this unpredictable, uncontrollable ride?

Take control of your emotions and tell your feelings how to feel. They have no choice but to follow instructions coming from the boss.

The "Super You."

Visualize the person you will become at your fullest. Everything you wish to become, imagine reaching those levels at their highest. Imagine the best possible outcome of your visions. Envision if you were to reach all of your goals as perfectly as you can state, and fulfill your potential and then some.

This vision is what we'll call The Super You. This is the version of you that exists when you extend yourself to the fullest, maximizing your efforts and potential.

I once read a book which included the following exercise:

Imagine you're walking down a street and you see another person coming, walking in your direction. As you two get closer you see that this is not some random stranger, it's you! It's the you five years (or ten years, or six weeks) from now, walking right up to you. What does he do? How does he carry himself? How does he walk and talk? How does he feel abut himself and his life?

The Super You represents you at 150% of your life's possibilities.

What's stopping you from becoming The Super You? What are the specific reasons why you cannot become exactly like the person walking towards you in the street, besides your own beliefs that you cannot?

Exactly: Nothing is stopping you.

Visualize Your Future.

Your future is an extension of your present -- whatever you're doing now plants the seeds for what you'll have, what you'll do and who you'll be in the future. Look at your present and think about where it is taking you. What do you see? Do you see what you want to become, where you want to go, the things you wish to be doing?

Visualization is a very powerful technique. The practice has been studied and proven to have powers to shape our futures, when we visualize something consistently and strongly enough. If you have a strong vision of your future success and can hold that vision in your mind, you're contributing to making it a reality. Of course you must take action also, but remember that thoughts beget words which beget actions. So your actions are directly flowing from whatever your thoughts are.

So when you find yourself unmoved by your current circumstance, imagine how that circumstance is shaping your future life. This could be the boring persistence that you'll need in the long run, or it could mean it's time to pivot to a new situation. Conversely, when your future seems bleak, take action to change your current position -- physically or mentally -- and alter the future you're envisioning.

People Will Always Criticize.

Nobody cares to criticize someone who is doing nothing. The most accomplished people have the most critics, because they are doing the most about which to be discussed.

The more you move forward and build up accomplishments, the more criticism you will face. Your critics are the people who see your achievements as a threat for whatever reason. You may be a threat to their position, to their ego, or to their self-esteem. Many times, that criticism comes from those beneath you who have not done or even attempted what you've done or are doing. But criticism can come from anywhere.

No matter the source, you have a solution.

There has never been a statue erected for a critic. Use their energy for your own purposes. Any negativity can be turned around and/or redirected. Use your critics to fuel you, giving you something to fight against, literally or figuratively. As an audience to watch you, your critics suffer with your every success: Success is the best revenge. Or, you can choose to simply ignore them -- what is ignored diminishes and fades away.

Persistence: Boring But Necessary.

Doing much of one task can and will be monotonous, especially when you're doing the same day-in and day-out. Your mind gets tired. Your body fatigues. But to master a skill this is exactly what it takes -- complete immersion in a task until every aspect becomes second nature.

Most people never master any skill in life because they lack the discipline to stick to a pursuit through the long, boring repetition required for mastery. Fatigue of the mind and body sets in and they move into some new, shiny, exciting activity, only to leave that one, too, when it gets boring.

You can be different.

Persistence, like having energy, or showing up every day, isn't a personality quirk or an obscure talent that only some people are born with. Persistence is a skill which you can choose to have and sharpen. Having the most of this skill is a simple equation. Choose a goal, or an area or task or job to focus on. Keep going at it no matter how long it takes or how much effort is necessary. You don't have to be the most skilled or gifted at it. Just outlast everyone around you and be the only one still standing.

Rewards follow this persistence.

Be, Do, Have.

The path to achievement.

The first step is to Be the person that would reach that achievement. You may need to change who you are as a person, which entails changes in your habits, your thought patterns, and your physical environment to be that new individual. To get to a new place in life, you begin by being a new person. You can initiate that process, right now, by making a conscious change in how you see and think about the world and yourself.

Once you've become (or set in motion to become) the person you needed to become, the second step is the actual doing -- taking the actions to get and do what you want with your life. This is the most time-consuming step and the most challenging. Many people quit during this phase when the doing gets monotonous or the waters are not so smooth. You know that nothing worthwhile comes easy in life. This Doing phase is the main course in your meal of achievement.

The final phase is you Having what you want. You become the person with your thoughts and habits, do what that person does to acquire the abilities, then you'll have the position or achievement you want.

Be it, Do it, Have it.

Dre Baldwin

Being Self-Generated.

In life, help can arrive in many forms; Sometimes expected, sometimes unexpected. People you know may lend a hand. Someone you don't know could swoop in out of nowhere and do something helpful for you. You may ask for help from someone and receive what you asked for. There may be someone who loves to help people who is looking for a person to help, and there you are. What great timing!

None of this should be counted on.

In life, the more you can depend on yourself, the more power and independence you'll have. If you have ever been in a dependent relationship, where one person needs the other for their survival, you know how weak and powerless you feel when you want something done but can't make it happen on your own. Nothing can happen until another person does this, this and that or gives the OK.

When you're self-reliant and solely dependent on your own power you don't need to wait or depend on outside forces to get things done for you, when you want them done and how you want them done. Any help is appreciated but not needed and never begged for. The paradoxical truth is that the more you help yourself, the more other people will look to help you and want to be a part of what you do. A desperate person begging for help has trouble finding it -- desperation repels people. Strength and power attracts.

It's great to have a support team around you -- you never know when someone else can offer what you

106

lack. None of us is great at everything. The spirit of the self-reliant mindset, though, is "I can do it or I will teach myself how." This state of mind will attract everything you'll need to make that thought true.

Erase The Bad Movies.

You've been to the movies many times, and you have your favorites. Also, you've probably seen a handful or terrible films that were just a waste of your time and money.

Would you pay to see those movies again? Of course not. Would you suggest them at a friend's house if they asked what you wanted to see? You would not.

So why do you, in your head, replay the bad movies -- the negative situations that start a flow of negative thinking, draining your energy and bringing your positive vibes down -- over and over again?

When you see a bad movie, you throw out the ticket stub, alert any friends who were thinking about seeing it, trash the film on your Facebook timeline, and forget that lost two hours of your life.

You don't watch bad movies twice. You would never pay to see those films again. You'd do your best to make sure your friends don't have to sit through them either; you would save them the time by letting them know that there are better options.

Do the same with all the bad movies of you life. Erase them. Delete the files off of your memory's hard drive and use that space for something new and uplifting.

Surround Yourself With People Who Can Help You.

Some of us are loners -- we spend a lot of time by ourselves, and are completely comfortable this way. Some people, though, like having other people around. If you're that type and you are going to have people in your circle that you spend ample time around, make sure they are the type of people who add to, and do not take away from, your purpose.

If you're running a business, people should be there to work. If they are friends, you should be able to count on them just as they can count on you. Synergy occurs when the whole is greater than the sum of its parts -- in simple terms, one plus one equals three when synergy is happening. When the people surrounding you are taking away from your purpose, one plus one equals some amount less than two. The parts are making the whole weaker.

How do you feel when the people in your circle come around? Do you feel energized and ready to achieve? Do you anticipate things getting bogged down? Do the people on your team make you feel like weight is lifted off of you, or do you feel having them puts more on you? Are they strong where you are weak? Do they supplement your best qualities or do you feel guilty about being yourself in their presence?

The people in your circle should serve to make you better and not worse. Adjust the circle as necessary.

You Learn by Doing, Over and Over.

Reading about the skills you want is a valuable tool. As has been said, if you want to hide something from people, put it in a book. There is valuable information to be learned from reading.

Watching others do things before you do them is good too; you can get a general grasp of the task, see what works and doesn't work for them and apply it to your future actions. You may see something you can remember and apply to your work later on.

The only way you'll really remember and really "know" how to do something, however, is to do it, and do it over and over, having that hands-on experience drilled into your mental and physical memory. You will eventually forget things that are said and observed. Your experiences -- actions you lived through -- stay with you forever.

Experience is, simply stated, the act of living through mistakes. An expert in any area becomes an expert only from doing, from experiencing every possible mistake in a field. You cannot get there from reading and watching. You must do, and fail, to gain experience. Those who have done so are the best teachers.

Your ability to show or explain to someone else how to do something will only be as valuable as your own experience in doing it yourself.

You "Need Help"?

This is the most helpless statement in the English language and it would do you well to extirpate it from your vocabulary.

If you are in a situation in which you aren't getting the results you wanted, what you need could be increased effort, more information, or a completely different approach. You absolutely cannot ever put yourself in a position mentally where you have decided that your only way out of a circumstance is to receive help from another person. Doing this renders you completely powerless in the mind, which will in turn conjure up its physical manifestation.

So let's say your toilet is clogged and flooding your bathroom. Am I saying not to call a plumber, who can fix it better and faster than you? The plumber would, after all, be helping you. This is not what I mean.

What I wish for you to grasp is the *spirit* of the principle (taking control and responsibility for yourself), not the *letter* of it ("I broke my leg and am refusing to see a doctor; Dre said 'No help!'").

Every one of us has our own concerns and issues to deal with daily -- the most able person you know or can name has her own issues that require her attention every day. Despite what you may think, there is not a soul alive who has unlimited time to dedicate to resolving your issues.

Waiting on help from others places you in a position of dependency (remember our discussion of self-reliance) and leaves you subject to the whims and feelings of other people. Is that what you want? There is no power and no future in that position.

When your current plan is not working, the only help you need is from yourself -- observe, think, then act. Be, Do and Have. You may, indeed, receive some outside help but it should all serve to supplement your best efforts, not to replace them.

You Already Have All You Need.

Wherever you want to go, whatever you want to do in life, you already have all you need to make it happen -- your health, your sharp mind, and a clear idea of what you want to do. You don't need more time, help from others, or currently inaccessible outside resources. Anything you want can be manifested from within.

You know what you want. You have a basic understanding of what it will take to get it. You can see it in your mind and, if you focus hard enough, you can feel what it will be like to have it, be it, do it.

The only thing stopping you from doing it is you, and whatever is in your mind telling you that you cannot. Everything you need is already within you, and everything stopping you from having or becoming it is also within you. Start making use of the former and you will destroy the latter.

You Don't Need More "How-To."

There are people who don't do things they want to do because they don't have an exact, step-by-step blueprint on what to do, how to do it and when. I know several people personally, who talk to me about things they wish to do, ideas they have, plans that they know they need to get started on. When I ask what the holdup is, many times I hear, "I just don't know how," or, "I don't know what to do."

News Flash: you will *never* know 100% of what to do before you begin anything in life. None of us would do anything if knowing everything was a requirement to begin. You will learn plenty as you go along, and make your adjustments. But if you never begin you will be stuck on the dock forever, talking about what you want to be doing or even worse, what you could have done.

When you give in to I-don't-know-enough-yet it becomes a habit. When you learn some new information, you want to wait until you get a little more. Every small bit you get, you want to wait for more and what you do know is never enough. On and on it goes, and before you know it, years have gone by and you've done nothing.

The smartest man in the world, they say, is the man that knows he knows nothing. We are always learning in our lives no matter our age or experience or position. Our world is constantly changing; you'll never have all the information. Learning happens when you're out in the world, moving. You can't learn from your parking spot.

Start the car now and let things go where they may.

Make The Difficult Easy, and The Easy Difficult.

Our most fatal mistakes usually occur when we come up on the easy parts in life. On the other end of this conundrum, we make life's challenges much more difficult than they really are in our heads, setting ourselves up for failure.

The solution to this is to perform the easy stuff as if it were the hard stuff -- increased focus, a stronger sense of urgency, attention to detail, no careless mistakes.

With the difficult tasks, perform them as if they are easy -- "do without doing," less over-thinking, allowing our minds and actions to flow freely, allowing our instincts to guide us rather than trying to be perfect or avoid mistakes.

You will find yourself making fewer careless errors in your most numerous tasks: The basic, easy stuff. With the difficult, challenging tasks, you'll have more flow and fluidity, and you won't psych yourself out of action anymore as you give your mind permission to relax and loosen up.

Know Everything About Your Work.

Whatever business or field you're in, it is your job to know all there is to know about it. If you're serious about and committed to your work, make it your job to be informed.

You do not need to be an expert in everything -- no one can be because and there is too much to know about too many things for this to be possible -- but you should know the basics of what's happening and what's supposed to be happening in your area of focus.

If you're dedicated to achieving a certain level of success in your business, you must stay connected. Connected to what is going on, connected to new information, and connected to what the people around you -- competition, past participants, future peers, and your own team -- are doing. This is all part of the job when you want to hold a top spot.

Help Others, It Will Come Back To You.

Every good thing eventually ends. Your life is one of those good things. Nothing you do, no items you've acquired, nothing you have on your person or in your pockets right now, can come with you. What will be left to represent your time on this earth when you're gone?

One thing that will live on is what you pass on to others. Material things are nice but they all eventually go away, wear out and/or get replaced. The knowledge and experience you pass along to the next generations lives on forever as it gets passed around and spreads to all who follow you.

We know the repellant effect of chasing things in life. To attract things, find a way to help someone else get what you want. If you think you could use some help on a task, seek out someone you can help, and see how your task miraculously becomes easier to complete.

Anything you want, find a way to help someone else get it and experience the state of "not-needing." Then things will come to you, instead of you having to seek and hunt things. Chase money and it gets harder and harder to make. Help some other people make money, and money will follow you everywhere you go.

Chase your shadow, it runs faster and faster away from you. Turn and walk away, though, and your shadow follows everywhere you go.

*I (Dre Baldwin) am a 31-year-old professional athlete, marketer, model, brand developer and author born and raised in Philadelphia, PA. After graduating with a business management and marketing degree from Penn State, I began blogging in 2005 and posting basketball workouts and motivational messages on YouTube in 2006. Since then I have seen over 2 million visitors to my personal website DreAllDay.com and been viewed over 22 million times on YouTube in over 3,000 videos. I published my first book **"Buy A Game"** in 2012.*

I currently reside in Miami, Florida.

Made in the USA
San Bernardino, CA
06 August 2017